TWEETABLE
AUGUSTINE

Infotainment Press

Tweetable Augustine: Quips, Quotes & Other One-Liners

Copyright © 2021 by Infotainment Press

All rights reserved. No portion of this book may be reproduced, stored in a retrieval system, or transmitted in any form or by any means—electronic, mechanical, photocopy, recording, scanning, or other—except for brief quotations in critical reviews or articles, without the prior written permission of the publisher.

Unless otherwise noted, Scripture quotations are taken from THE HOLY BIBLE, KING JAMES VERSION.

TWEETABLE AUGUSTINE

QUIPS, QUOTES & OTHER ONE-LINERS

*E*ssentially, there are two kinds of people, because there are two kinds of love. One is subject to God; the other endeavors to equal him.

*U*nless humility will precede, accompany, and follow up all the good we accomplish, pride will snatch everything right out of our hands.

*T*he love of drunkenness arouses a hatred of truth.

*S*erving God is a great benefit to humanity.
   By commanding, God makes his wishes beneficial; there is no fear that what he orders is harmful.

If anyone seems to have acted well, he should not be said to have acted rightly unless he acted out of the duty which has God as its object.

The honors of this world, what are they but puff, and emptiness, and peril of falling?

The man who cannot speak both eloquently and wisely should speak wisely without eloquence, rather than eloquently without wisdom.

How high a price we pay for the burden of habit!

He who made all things is better than all things. Love the Creator in his creature and the maker in what he has made.

Let us ask God not to deprive us of our prayer and his mercy so that we pray with perseverance and he may have mercy with his perseverance.

Holy Spirit, descend plentifully into my heart. Enlighten the dark corners of this neglected dwelling and scatter there Your cheerful beams.

Our Lord Jesus Christ was not only born of the everlasting God, but was also now born from the Holy Ghost, of the Virgin Mary.

How sure, unchangeable and effectual is the will of God. Nothing happens but by His will either permitting it to be done or Himself doing it

Show me a lover and he will understand what I am saying.

Christ is not valued at all, unless he is valued above all.

A servant of sin is free to sin and will not be free to do right until, being freed from sin, he begins to be the servant of righteousness.

For instantly, as the sentence ended, there was in my heart a full certainty and all the gloom of doubt vanished away.

To wisdom belongs the intellectual apprehension of things eternal; to knowledge, the rational apprehension of things temporal.

Pornography deadens the heart.

The law detects. Grace alone conquers sin.

God is man's happiness.

You are filled and you are empty. Fill your empty neighbor from your fullness, so that your emptiness may be filled from God's fullness.

Patience is the companion of wisdom.

Those same things then troubled me, which now in quiet security I am proposing and explaining to you in the Name of the Lord.

Every day my conscience makes confession, relying on the hope of Your mercy as more to be trusted than its own innocence.

The prayers of the Church have been heard, and the kings have become Christian, and you see now fulfilled what was then spoken in figure.

And yet the wife is subject to the husband, because it is fitting that she should be.

God knows what is better for us. Let us seek only that our heart be free from sin.

Now in the secure quiet of peace, the Churches might be built up, and peoples planted in the garden of God.

Some are peacemakers in themselves. By subjecting to reason all the motions of their souls they become themselves a kingdom of God.

The health of the soul is to cling steadfastly to the unchangeable God.

The only cause of evil is the falling away from the unchangeable good of a being made good but changeable.

Will is to grace as the horse is to the rider.

The Lord doth not say that he who beginneth shall be saved, "But he that endureth unto the end shall be saved."

From you, O God, come all good things, and from you, my God, comes all my salvation.

Charity is no substitute for justice withheld.

The Trinity is proof that God is love; for love requires the presence of a lover, a beloved, and the spirit of Love between them.

No knowledge of letters is more interior to us than that written in conscience: that one do to another what he himself doesn't want to suffer.

This also which follows they like to laugh at, she was found with Child of the Holy Ghost.

When we ask how good a man is, we do not ask what he does, nor even what he believes, but what he loves.

It is true that these lesser things have their delight, but none like my God, the maker of all things.

*L*ord, I will not quit until you gather all fragments of myself from my deformity, and unite them for eternity into the peace of our homeland

*D*o you aspire to great things? Begin with little ones.

*T*hat our Lord Jesus Christ might do this, He became the Son of man by being born of a woman.

*C*ommunity emerges only when we work to strengthen the values we share.

*P*ride does its own will;
> humility does the will of God.

If you believe what you like in the gospels,
and reject what you don't like, it is not
the gospel you believe, but yourself.

Christ loved us in our unloveliness, in order to make us beautiful like himself.

I judge God to be actually infinite, such that nothing whatsoever can be added to his perfection.

It was pride that changed angels into devils; it is humility that makes men as angels.

*F*orgiveness is the remission of sins. For it is by this that what has been lost, and was found, is saved from being lost again.

I became evil for no reason. I had no motive for my wickedness except wickedness itself. It was foul, and I loved it.

*Y*ou must be emptied of that which you are full, that you may be filled with that which you are empty.

*C*ome, Lord, and act. Rouse and renew us, kindle us and carry us away, shine before us and be gentle with us, let us love and run toward you.

In heaven we shall see, love, and praise. Our vision will never fail, our love will never end, and our praise will never fall silent.

The measure of love is to love without measure.

Conscience and reputation are two things. Conscience is due to yourself, reputation to your neighbor.

It is through things giving way to and taking the place of another that the beautiful tapestry of the ages is woven.

The will doesn't attain grace by freedom but freedom by
grace, and a delightful constancy and fortitude that it
may persevere.

It did not say, "He was subject to His mother,"
but "He was subject to them." To whom was
He subject? Was it not to His parents?

Life is grace.

The man who doesn't love believes in vain, even if his
beliefs are true; and hopes in vain even if the object
of his hope is true happiness.

*I*n my deepest wound I saw your glory, and it dazzled me.

If you long to be what you are not, you must always be displeased by what you are. Where you are pleased with yourself there you will remain.

All that's set forth in the sacraments of salvation refers to the hope of future good, than to retaining or attaining of present blessings.

Thou hast made us for thyself, O Lord, and our heart is restless until it finds its rest in thee.

The ultimate goal of the human mind is to know God.

Lord, whatever you give me is too little for me. Be you yourself my inheritance! Of what value is anything you give me that is not yourself?

We know too much, and are convinced of too little. Our literature is a substitute for religion, and so is our religion.

I forsook you, and I followed after your lowest creatures, I who was dust, turning to the dust.

Let abuses not be done away by harsh or autocratic measures but by teaching rather than by commanding, by persuasion rather than by threats.

With you there is true rest untroubled. He who enters in you enters into the joy of his Lord and shall possess his soul most happily in you.

Hold fast to Christ. For you He became temporal so that you might partake of eternity.

Beauty grows in you to the extent that love grows, because charity itself is the soul's beauty.

Unless our faith has its roots within a community it will not attain full fruition.

I intend to remind myself of my past foulness and carnal corruptions, not because I love them but so that I may love you, my God.

*T*here is no saint without a past,
no sinner without a future.

*W*hat jewel in their diadem is more precious than the Cross of Christ on the foreheads of kings?

I realize what I am and praise you for it. Come to my aid, that I may not stray from the way of salvation.

A good man pure in heart will not step aside from the truth for the sake of pleasing men or to avoid the annoyances which beset this life.

With love for mankind, and hatred of sins.

O death, when you seized my Lord,
  you then lost your grip on me.

Who is so foolishly curious that he would send his son to school in order to learn what the teacher thinks?

There are two things on account of which God loves his creation: in order that it should be and in order that it should abide.

For what am I to myself without You, but a guide to my own downfall?

You must not imagine that you are being drawn against your will, for the mind can also be drawn by love.

It is true that these lesser things have their delight, but none like my God, the maker of all things.

*L*ive as though Christ were coming today,
and you will not fear his coming.

*I*t's a height out of proportion to our state to leave God to whom the soul should cling as its basis and to become in some way our own basis.

*D*ost thou say that the same man is both the Son of David, and the Son of Abraham?

*E*nlighten the dark corners of this neglected dwelling and scatter there Thy cheerful beams.

*P*urity of life has reference to the love of God and one's neighbor; soundness of doctrine to the knowledge of God and one's neighbor.

Lord be our strong support from childhood to old age. When our strength is yours, we are strong. But when our strength is ours, we are weak.

The words printed here are concepts. You must go through the experiences.

There is in man a deep so deep it is hidden even to him in whom it is.

O Lord, grant me purity, but not yet.

You (God) have not only commanded continence, from what we are to restrain our love, but also justice, on what we are to bestow our love.

What is attended with difficulty in the seeking gives greater pleasure in the finding.

He who doesn't believe his sins can be pardoned, falls into despair and becomes worse as if no greater good remained for him than to be evil.

Without God, what am I but a guide to my own destruction?

*L*ord only this do I ask of your great kindness: that you convert me totally to you and let no obstacle to hinder me as I wend my way to you.

*H*ow clear an assent doth that your godly murmur convey!

*N*o eulogy is due to him who simply does his duty and nothing more.

*T*his church is the house of our prayers but we are the house of God. We are built up during life that we may be dedicated at the end of time.

*H*e hath subjected all powers,
He hath subjugated kings.

*L*et them therefore observe how they are mistaken who think that our seeking, asking, knocking is of ourselves and is not a gift given to us.

*I*t occurs at Mass when we say: "Forgive us our trespasses" so with a clean face we approach the table to receive Christ's Body and Blood.

*T*he hairs of his head are easier by far to count than his feeling, the movements of his heart.

*S*hame is the fear of losing pleasure when the good opinion of men gives more pleasure than the righteousness which leads a man to penitence.

O Lord, my God! I may imagine myself to be ever so just, but when you bring forth your treasury and apply it to me, I am found to be evil.

What you are must always displease you, if you are to attain to that which you are not.

In loving Him you will never be ashamed.

Great art Thou, O Lord, great is Thy power, and of thy wisdom there is no end. And man, being a part of thy creation, desires to praise Thee.

Whatever lacked Christ's name, no matter how learned and polished and veracious it was, could not wholly capture me.

A man is drawn by Christ, when he delights in truth, in blessedness, in holiness and in eternal life.

You are the life-giving pleasure of a pure heart.

To what place can I invite You since I am in You? Or where do You come from? To what place outside heaven and earth could I travel?

By faithfulness we're collected and wound up into unity within ourselves. Whereas we'd been scattered abroad in multiplicity.

The confession of evil works is the first beginning of good works.

Repentant tears wash out the stain of guilt.

But by being born of a woman, He purposed to show to us some high mystery.

*L*et them see how many orators, and scientific men, and philosophers of this world, have been caught by those fishermen.

*S*o stand with Him and you shall not fall; rest in Him and peace shall be yours.

*B*ut if I am talking to someone without any feeling, he will not know what I am talking about.

*W*e are Christians, and strangers on earth. Let none of us be frightened; our native land is not in this world.

Since you cannot do good to all, you are to pay special attention to those who are brought into closer connection with you.

If you want to be upright of heart, do not be displeased, over anything at all, with God.

I, wretch that I was, as thinking myself fit to fly, left the nest, and fell down before I flew.

Apostasy from God brings death to the soul.

Seek not to understand that you may believe,
but believe that you may understand.

What is done through fear of punishment or carnal motive, and has not for its principle the love of God, is not done as it ought to be done.

I was in love with loving.

A thing is not necessarily true because badly uttered, nor false because spoken magnificently.

You look kindly on the humble, but the lofty-minded You regard from afar. You draw close to those whose hearts are crushed.

*H*ope has two Daughters. Anger and Courage;
Anger at the way things are, and Courage
to see that they do not remain the way they are.

A bad will is one that is inordinately disposed to prefer
lower goods to higher ones.

*W*e must fly to our beloved homeland. There the
Father is and there is everything.

I do not see how I can say that even those who died in
their mother's womb shall have no resurrection.

*B*reathe in me. Act in me. Draw my heart. Strengthen me. Guard me. O Holy Spirit, that I always may be holy.

*B*e assured that all your diseases will be healed. There is no disease that the Almighty Physician cannot cure.

*H*abit, if not resisted, soon becomes necessity.

*P*unishment is justice for the unjust.

The capacity to have faith and to have love, belongs to men's nature; but to have faith and to have love, belongs to the grace of believers.

Doubtless there is a great mystery here: and glad are we, and we give thanks unto the Lord.

Set before my face all my perverse wanderings, that I may see them and hate them.

For the same reason again, women were the first who announced to the Apostles the Resurrection of God.

$\mathcal{L}$et those who read the Scriptures,
    remember this as we do;
    and let those who do not,
    give us credit.

Who will reflect on his weakness and dare credit his chastity to his own powers, so as to love you less as if having no need for your mercy?

Thanks be to Him who is desired before he is seen, whose presence is felt, and who is hoped for in the future.

The greatest of all alms is to forgive our debtors and to love our enemies.

God has promised forgiveness to your repentance, but He has not promised tomorrow to your procrastination.

No one ought to consider anything as his own,
except perhaps what is false. All truth is
of Him who says, I am the truth.

To sing is the work of a lover.

Divine Master, Grant that I may not so much seek to
be consoled, as to console; To be understood as to
understand; To be loved as to love.

The first woman whom God made, was called a woman
before she "knew" her husband.

You never go away from us, yet we have difficulty in returning to You. Come, Lord, stir us up and call us back.

Attend then to the generations of Christ, which Matthew has set down.

Lord, you are my helper and the helper of anyone who reaches out to you, my Redeemer, for the very purpose of enabling me to reach out to you.

On our journey, we must live where Christ is in need. He is needy in his followers, for he himself has no needs.

*B*ehold my heart my God. Look inside and cleanse it of disordered affection by directing my eyes to you and lifting my feet out of the snare.

*T*he desire is thy prayers; and if thy desire is without ceasing, thy prayer will also be without ceasing.

*H*e who made His disciples fishers of men, enclosed within His nets every kind of authority.

*A*ll other sins only prevail in evil deeds; pride only has to be guarded against in things that are rightly done.

Judas betrayed Him. God then both delivers the nations by the Passion of His Son, and punishes Judas for his own wickedness.

A little way back women received their precepts. Now let children receive theirs—to obey their parents, and to be subject to them.

We await with hope the resurrection of the body to eternal glory.

Greatness is all the more admirable if it is achieved against odds.

*E*very approach to a good and blessed life is to be found in the true religion.

I pray to God who no one lets go unless deceived; who no one seeks unless taught and who no one finds unless cleansed. Come mercifully to me.

*E*arthly riches are full of poverty.

I want my friend to miss me as long as I miss him.

A good man, though a slave, is free;
but a wicked man, though a king,
is a slave.

$\mathcal{L}$ord, I am poor and needy. I'm better only when with heartfelt sorrow I renounce myself and seek your mercy and my deficiencies are overcome.

$\mathcal{C}$omplete abstinence is easier than perfect moderation.

$\mathcal{I}$t is not enough to be drawn of your own free will, because you can be drawn by delight as well.

$\mathcal{L}$ove God and do whatever you please: for the soul trained in love to God will do nothing to offend the One who is Beloved.

He who enters into you enters in the joy of his Lord,
and he shall have no fear, and he shall possess his
soul most happily in him who is the supreme good.

The only cause of any good that we enjoy
is the goodness of God.

He who truly knows how to live rightly is he
who rightly knows how to pray.

A man who does not strive about words, uses words
with no other purpose than to make the truth plain,
pleasing, and effective.

Leave room for reflection and silence. Enter into yourself and leave behind all noise. Hear the word in quietness that you may understand it.

"But now, would He have been any less a man, if He had not been born of the Virgin Mary," one may say.

Is it any merit to abstain from wine if one is intoxicated with anger?

I have learnt to love you late, Beauty at once so ancient and so new!

Your desires are your prayers; and if your desire is without ceasing, your prayer should be without ceasing.

O Holy Spirit, descend plentifully into my heart. Enlighten the dark corners of this neglected dwelling and scatter there Thy cheerful beams.

Lord, see your work in me, not my own. For if you see my own work, you condemn me; but if you see yours, you crown me.

He who is filled with love is filled with God himself.

*G*od loves each of us
   as if there were only one of us.

Walking by faith, let us do good works. In these let there be a free love of God for his own sake and an active love for our neighbor.

To abstain from sin when one can no longer sin is to be forsaken by sin, not to forsake it.

Anything erroneous found in these writings is the only thing to be attributed to me, while anything that is true comes from the one God.

He is drawn by the things he is running to take, drawn because he desires . . . drawn simply by the pull on his appetite.

A just man made from a sinner is greater than to create the world, the world will pass but the justification of the sinner will endure.

He that is jealous is not in love.

The soul is torn apart in a painful condition as long as it prefers the eternal, but does not discard the temporal because of familiarity.

Joseph is told, "He is of the Holy Ghost;" and yet his paternal authority is not taken from him.

The Son is Light from Light yet we cannot claim to be light by nature, but we are illuminated from that Light so that we can shine in wisdom.

O Lord, who teachest by sorrow, and woundest us, to heal; and killest us, lest we die from Thee.

All who love the world dwell in it by their love, just as all whose hearts are lifted upward dwell by their love in heaven.

The veils make that which is kept secret honored . . . because then we "turn unto Christ, the veil is taken away."

He who speaks wisely and eloquently but lives wickedly, may instruct many who are anxious to learn; though, he is unprofitable to himself.

Narrow is the mansion of my soul; enlarge it, that you may enter in. It is ruinous; repair it.

I look forward, not to what lies ahead of me in this life and will surely pass away, but to my eternal goal.

Why are you relying on yourself, only to find yourself unreliable?

In this was my sin, that not in him but in his creatures, in myself and others, did I seek pleasure, honors and truths.

What thief puts up with another thief with a calm mind?

Mark then, holy brethren, the usefulness of heretics.

God, although nothing worthy of His greatness can be said of Him, has condescended to accept the worship of men's mouths.

We'll soon celebrate the passion of our Lord. It is our commitment to him that we should restrain the desires of the flesh.

Don't you believe that there is in man a deep so profound as to be hidden even to him in whom it is?

When God rewards us for our labor, He is only crowning His work in us.

It is certain that it is we that will when we will, but it is He who makes us will what is good.

*L*ord, you strengthened me because I took refuge in you; and I took refuge because you freed me.

It is you I desire, O Justice and Innocence, beautiful and comely in full light. Great peace is with you, as is untroubled life.

Yes, if we live religiously, if we believe Christ they only bring us to this—to the knowledge of mysteries.

The mind commands the body and is instantly obeyed. The mind orders the mind yet it does not perform.

I acknowledge you, O Lord, in your humility, that I may not fear you in your glory. For to those who desire you, you come in clemency.

O my soul, why are you so distracted by things? Why are you so occupied with earthly and mortal cares? Stay with me and praise the Lord!

I do not condemn the creature which I made.

*W*hen a man is out of the right way the more quickly and impetuously he advances, the more he errs.

*B*eauty is indeed a good gift of God; but that the good may not think it a great good, God dispenses it even to the wicked.

In a cornerstone you see the end of one wall, the beginning of another; therefore the cornerstone which connects both walls is reckoned twice.

It is one of the distinctive features of good intellects not to love words, but the truth in words.

The Bible was composed in such a way that as beginners mature, its meaning grows with them.

What God commands to be done would not be asked for from God, unless it could be given by Him that it should be done.

Lord, you are my helper that I may dwell in your love, my redeemer that you may deliver me from my wrongdoing.

We would not love God unless He first loved us. Hence the words of our Lord to His disciples: You have not chosen me but I have chosen you.

For grace is given not because we have done good works, but in order that we may be able to do them.

Wretch that I am, do I dare to say that you, my God, were silent when in reality I was traveling farther from you?

*Y*ou have made us for Yourself,
   and our hearts are restless
      until they find their rest in You.

The Truth, clad in flesh, came healed through his flesh
the inner eye of our heart, that afterward we might
be able to see him face to face.

You say, the times are troublesome. Live rightly and you
will change the times. Change human beings and the
times will be changed.

An eternal object is loved with greater ardor when it is
in possession than while it is still an object of desire.

Thou must be emptied of that wherewith
thou art full, that thou mayest be filled
with that whereof thou art empty.

A miserable slavery of the soul is to take signs for things and not set the eye of the mind above the corporeal and into eternal light.

Hate the sin, love the sinner.

Both the beginning of faith in the Lord and continuance in the Lord unto the end, are God's gifts.

God is always trying to give good things to us, but our hands are too full to receive them.

May God then be with you, and give you grace with
gentle persuasiveness to report your spectacles to
your friends.

The world is a book, and those who do not travel read
only a page.

Let no one then reproach Christ with His birth
of a woman.

The soul enjoys nothing in freedom except
what it enjoys in peace.

The light of our understandings, by which all things are learned by us, have affirmed to be that selfsame God by whom all things were made.

He loves Thee too little, who loves anything together with Thee, which he loves not for Thy sake.

It is well known then, that "Jesus" in the Hebrew tongue is in Latin interpreted "Savior."

For if you were to behold nothing, you would hear nothing.

When these things are read of in the church,
you behold them with pleasure with these eyes
of the heart.

The wicked do not go alone,
but the saints also go with them.

Christ the humble would not have taught His mother
to be proud.

He who created us without our help will not save us
without our consent.

$\mathcal{W}$hoever loves his neighbor aright, ought to urge upon him that he too should love God with his whole heart, and soul, and mind.

$\mathcal{L}$et us pray, dearly beloved, that the God of grace may give even to our enemies, to understand that no one is delivered save by God's grace.

$\mathcal{A}$ temporal object is valued more before possessed and begins to prove worthless the moment we attain it since it does not satisfy the soul.

$\mathcal{T}$o your grace and mercy I ascribe it that you have dissolved my sins as if they were ice. To your grace I ascribe any evil I have not done.

*T*here is something in humility
    which strangely exalts the heart.

The soul fornicates when it turns away from you and, apart from you, seeks pure things as it does not find except when it returns to you.

Beg God for the gift to love one another, love all people, even your enemy. Not because he is your brother, but that he may become such.

What I desire for all my works, of course, is not merely a kind reader but also a frank critic.

The world was subject unto Christ, and Christ was subject to His parents.

It's not by change of place that we can come nearer to Him who is in every place, but by the cultivation of pure desires and virtuous habits.

For I am aware what ability is requisite to persuade the proud how great is the virtue of humility.

Give me strength to seek you, Lord, for you have already enabled me to find you and have given me hope of finding you ever more fully.

We make ourselves a ladder out of our vices if we trample the vices themselves underfoot.

The peace of the celestial city is the perfectly ordered and harmonious enjoyment of God, and of one another in God.

If we live good lives, the times are also good. As we are, such are the times.

Without the Spirit man's will is not free, since it has been laid under by shackling and conquering desires.

The face of God will give insatiable satisfaction of which we will not tire.

*D*raw my heart, O Holy Spirit, that I may love only
what is holy. Strengthen me, O Holy Spirit,
that I may defend all that is holy.

*W*ithout You, what am I to myself but a guide to my
own self-destruction?

*P*ride is the beginning of an evil will. Pride is the desire
of a height out of proportion to our state.

*Y*ou called and shouted and burst my deafness.
You flashed, shone, and scattered my blindness.

*T*he free choice of the will is the reason
    why we do wrong and suffer
    Your just judgment.

We are more inclined to reply to arguments that oppose our error, than to see how happy would be our condition if we were free from error.

God's knowledge is not like ours, which has 3 tenses: present, past, and future. His knowledge has no change or variation.

As to His Divine Nature He is before all times, and without time.

For the Captain suffered Himself to be tried, only that He might teach His soldier to fight.

There are two causes of sin: either we do not know our
duty or we do not perform the duty that we know.
We need God's help to overcome both.

Hence, my brethren, understand the sense
of Scripture . . . whose sole design in their
marriage was to have children by their wives.

The Word of God is never silent,
though it is not always heard.

Do not refuse to regain your youth in Christ who says:
The world is passing away. Do not fear. Your youth
shall be renewed.

You are not told: Be less than you are; but know what you are. Know that you are a sinful human, that it's God who frees you from blame.

There is a certain desire of the heart to which the bread of heaven appeals.

Lord, heal and open my eyes that I may recognize your will. Put to flight my foolishness that I may know you.

With your word you pierced my heart, and I loved you. But heaven and earth and everything in them on all sides tell me to love you.

To fall in love with God is the greatest of all romances;
to seek him, the greatest adventure; to find him,
the greatest human achievement.

Love is the only sign that distinguishes the children
of God from the children of the devil.

Do not go outside, go back into yourself,
the heart of the creature lives in the truth.

The greatest evil is physical pain.

This is our faith, that this we profess and confess;
for this faith thousands of martyrs have been
slain in all the world.

Necessity has no law.

Lord, show me the way I must travel that I may see you.

Right is right even if no one is doing it;
wrong is wrong even if everyone is doing it.

The poison to deceive man was presented him
  by woman, through woman let salvation
  for man's recovery be presented.

A grand spectacle to the eyes of the heart doth a whole
  mind in a mangled body exhibit!

We cannot pass our guardian angel's bounds, resigned
  or sullen, he will hear our sighs.

This then we religiously believe, this most firmly hold
  fast, that Christ was born by the Holy Ghost
  of the Virgin Mary.

O Lord, deliver me from this lust
of always vindicating myself.

*L*ord Jesus you suffered for us not yourself. You bore the punishment for no fault of your own, to abolish both the fault and the punishment.

*H*e that is kind is free, though he is a slave; he that is evil is a slave, though he be a king.

*T*he woman in Paradise announced death to her husband, and the women in the Church announced salvation to the men.

*I*t is not the punishment but the cause that makes the martyr.

As man fell through pride God restored him through
   humility. Ensnared by the wisdom of the serpent
   he is set free by the foolishness of God.

Let me die, lest I die.

Instruct me, Lord, and command what You will.
   But first heal me and open my ears
   that I may hear Your words.

O God in you there is no strife, no disorder, no change,
   no need, no death but supreme harmony, supreme
   clarity, supreme permanence and life.

Let my soul take refuge beneath the shadow of your wings: let my heart, this sea of restless waves, find peace in you O God!

This is my glory, Lord my God, that I may proclaim to you that there is nothing from myself for me. All good things come from you.

As our body cannot live without nourishment, so our soul cannot live without prayer.

To seek the highest good is to live well.

My thoughts are torn this way and that in the havoc
of change. So it will be until I am purified
by the fire of Your love.

Beautiful is the modest mind that admits
its own limitations.

The punishment of every disordered mind
is its own disorder.

Since love grows within you, so beauty grows.
For love is the beauty of the soul.

*T*his is the very perfection of a man,
 to find out his own imperfections.

Understanding is the reward of faith. Therefore seek not to understand that you may believe, but believe that you may understand.

Miracles are not contrary to nature, but only contrary to what we know about nature.

Let not the husband go to any other woman,
nor the woman to any other man,
for from this adultery gets its name.

There is no way whereby any person arrives at perfection or makes progress to true and godly righteousness but the assisting grace of Christ.

By my irregular life I shut the gate of my Lord against myself: when I should have knocked for it to be opened.

For as He could be born of a woman without a man, so could He also have been born without the woman.

What poisonous food does for the body, is what inducement to wickedness does for the soul.

Grace does not destroy the will but rather restores it.

I call upon you, my God. Come into my soul, which you have prepared for your own reception by inspiring in me a longing for your goodness.

*H*is body was lifted up on the Cross, and so He subdued souls to the Cross.

*A*s a lamp does not light itself, so the human soul does light itself but calls out to God: You indeed, O Lord, give light to my lamp.

I dared to search in pride for that which none but the humble can discover.

*T*wo cities are formed by two loves: the earthly by the love of self and contempt of God, the heavenly by the love of God and contempt of self.

*A*ttend, dearly beloved, and see what wholesome advice the Apostle gives.

*L*et each sex then at once see its honor, and confess its iniquity, and let them both hope for salvation.

A man speaks with more or less wisdom just as he has made more or less progress in the knowledge of Scripture.

Grace makes us lovers of the law; but the law itself,
> without grace, makes us nothing but breakers
> of the law.

For what is the self-complacent man but a slave
> to his own self-praise.

The spiritual virtue of a sacrament is like light—
> although it passes among the impure,
> it is not polluted.

Believe and you will understand;
> faith precedes, follows intelligence.

By the evil use of his free-will man destroyed both it and himself. Sin being victorious over him, the freedom of his will was lost.

If God is to be loved more than any man, each man ought to love God more than himself.

O God, come to me in your kindness. You are the good and the beautiful, in whom, by whom and through whom all things are good and beautiful.

What the soul is in our body, the Holy Spirit is in the body of Christ.

*T*he desire for happiness is essential
to humans and is the motive
of all our actions.

We must beware of the man who abounds in eloquent nonsense and not think that because the speaker is eloquent what he says must be true.

Lord, because of your Name have mercy in me and by no means abandon the work you have begun but complete what is imperfect in me.

Alas for me, O Lord, how high you are in the heights, and how deep in the depths! Nowhere do you withdraw, yet we scarcely return to you!

No persons live justly unless they have been made just; and humans are made just by him who can never be unjust.

Let everyone's sighs be uttered in longing for Christ, since the all-beautiful One loves repulsive people so that he may make them beautiful.

The crucifixion is something that continues throughout our life, not for forty days only.

Crimes, however great, may be remitted by the mercy of God. Forgiveness is never to be despaired of by men who truly repent.

For what does it have an insatiable appetite, unless it is that it may eat and drink wisdom, righteousness, truth and eternal life?

If you do not want to fear, probe your inmost self. Does not a poisoned vein of the wasting love of the world still pulse there?

The beard is a masculine ornament, given to us by God not for any practical use, but for our dignity.

And they, turning their thoughts to Christ, have run to the church, have overcome, not any man, but the devil himself.

There is no love without hope, no hope without love, and neither love nor hope without faith.

Happiness is joy in the truth because it is joy in you,
O Lord, who are truth, my light, my salvation,
my God.

Nothing whatever pertaining to godliness and real
holiness can be accomplished without grace.

Lust is the affection of the mind which aims at enjoying
one's self and one's neighbor and other earthly
things, without reference to God.

Does not Christ draw when he is revealed to us
by the Father? What does the mind desire more
eagerly than truth?

*B*ecause of our sins we are in darkness; but you, my God, will illuminate my darkness.

Lord, you look kindly on what is humble, but
   the lofty-minded you regard from afar. Only
   to those whose hearts are crushed do you draw close.

There cannot be love of God in someone who does not
   love his neighbor, there cannot be love of neighbor in
   someone who does not love God.

You never abandon what You have begun.
   Make perfect my imperfections.

Charity is the affection of the mind which aims at
   enjoying God for His own sake and one's self and
   one's neighbor in subordination to God.

O Lord, my God, you alone do I love. You alone am I prepared to serve, for you alone justly rule, and under your authority I long to be.

*J*ust as in the case of Judas; what great good did he! By the Lord's Passion all nations are saved.

*H*ow then shall I find you, if I do not remember you?

I asked the whole frame of the world about my God; and he answered, I am not He, but He made me.

When the soul rules and animates the body it does not become tainted from that fact, but only when it starts to lust after transitory things.

Hesitate not then to reckon the head of the corner twice, and you have at once the number written.

Men go abroad to admire the heights of mountains, yet pass over the mystery of themselves without a thought.

God judged it better to bring good out of evil than to suffer no evil to exist.

$\mathcal{J}$ust as no one can exist of himself, so no one can be wise of himself, but only by the enlightening influence of God.

$\mathcal{T}$he very desire with which you want to understand is itself a prayer to God.

$\mathcal{Y}$ou are my Lord, because You have no need of my goodness.

$\mathcal{S}$o, brethren, you believe it in all assurance; you have no cause to blush for it.

Lord, help us, so that a change may be achieved in us, and we may find you ready to offer yourself for the enjoyment of those you love you.

You aspire to great things? Begin with little ones.

Order your soul; reduce your wants; live in charity; associate in Christian community; obey the laws; trust in Providence.

Heaven outshines Rome.

Don't be so given to contemplation that you give no thought to your neighbor nor so given to activity to allow no time contemplating God.

No sinner is to be loved as a sinner; and every man is to be loved as a man for God's sake; but God is to be loved for His own sake.

Whosoever prays from the Lord that he may persevere in good, confesses thereby that such perseverance is His gift.

Seeking a rational explanation for the origin of sin is like trying to see darkness or hear silence.

*I*nstead of victory, truth;
>   instead of high rank, holiness;
>   instead of peace, felicity;
>   instead of life, eternity.

*L*ord, those are your best servants who wish to shape their life on your answers rather than shape your answers to their wishes.

*M*an's iniquity lies to itself whether by corrupting their own nature, which you have made, or by an immoderate use of things given to men.

I vacillate between the peril of pleasure and the value of experience.

O Lord, the happy life is this: to rejoice to Thee, in Thee, and for Thee!

You, who believe what you please, and reject what you please, believe yourselves or your own fancy rather than the Gospel.

Pride is the love of one's own superiority, while jealousy is the hatred of another good fortune.

A man who says what is false thinking that it is true, is better than the one who says what is true but in his conscience intends to deceive.

Let both the woman and the man seek relief for their infirmity in themselves.

Lord, I am better only when with heartfelt sorrow I renounce myself and seek your mercy so that my deficiencies are overcome and transformed.

Hear how He hath told us Himself, and foretold it before He was made a spectacle.

If we did not have rational souls, we would not be able to believe.

The people who remained victorious were less like conquerors than conquered.

God examines both rich and poor, not according to their lands and houses, but according to the riches of their hearts.

Lower goods have their delights, but none such as my God, for in him the just man finds delight, and he is the joy of the upright of heart.

An express clause is there that they marry "for the procreation of children;" and this is called the marriage contract.

We must think and believe that whatever is written in the Scriptures is better and truer than anything we could devise by our own wisdom.

*G*od had one son on earth without sin,
but never one without suffering.

It is in giving that we receive; It is in pardoning
   that we are pardoned; And it is in dying
   to ourselves that we are born to eternal life.

When any freeman goes to an astrologer, he gives
   money that he may come away the slave either
   of Mars or of Venus.

Even though I grieve that I do not see you, I take some
   comfort in my pain. And in this sweet yearning
   I seek some small consolation.

I found thee not, O Lord, without, because I erred in
   seeking thee without that wert within.

Lord, my God, how great you are, yet you make your
 home in the humble of heart! You lift up the
 downtrodden, and you are their grandeur.

Come, Lord, into my soul, which you have prepared
 for your own reception by inspiring in me
 a longing for your goodness.

When God is our strength, it is strength indeed;
 when our strength is our own, it is only weakness.

Job counted God's will his treasure, nor did it grieve him
 to lose those earthly goods which we all must soon
 lose at our death.

Love all men equally. But since you can't do good to all, pay special regard to those who by circumstance are in closer connection with you.

Unless you believe, you will not understand.

The house of my soul, O LORD, lies in ruins . . . rebuild it.

The world must be used not enjoyed, that by means of what is material and temporary we may lay hold upon that which is spiritual and eternal.

He departed from our sight that we might return to our heart, and there find Him. For He departed, and behold, He is here.

Find out how much God has given you and from it take what you need; the remainder is needed by others.

This man emphasizes how high above you Christ has been lifted up; Christ, though, says how low he came down to you.

He abstains from evil who prevents sin to have dominion over him and when evil thought comes over him suffers it not to come to actual deed.

You who are fervent in spirit, be enkindled with the fire of love. Let your lives glow with the praises of God and irreproachable lives.

They who make gods of the works of man have sunk lower than they who make gods of the works of God.

For what thief will suffer a thief? Even a rich thief will not suffer him who is driven to it by want.

Every being, even if it be a defective one, in so far as it is a being is good, and in so far as it is defective is evil.

A extravagant perversity is in the self-love of a man who desires others to be in error that the fact of his having erred may not be found.

*I*n proportion as the dominion of lust is pulled down, in the same proportion is that of charity built up.

*E*ducated Christians like me expect God's grace to prefer those of greater ability and education. God mocks my expectations.

*C*ommand, Lord, and requisition whatever you wish. But heal and open my ears so that I may hear your voice.

*M*an wishes to be happy
even when he so lives
as to make happiness impossible.

*E*xalted is the homeland, and humble is the way.
The homeland is the life of Christ, and his death
is the way.

*P*ray lest we fall to temptation. They deny this who claim
grace is not needed to avoid sin and that the will that
knows the law is sufficient

O Lord, I love you. I love, I burn, I pant for you;
I trample under foot all that gives here delight.
I want to go to you.

*L*ord, I have waited for you to come and deliver me from
every need. For in my need you have not forsaken
your law of mercy.

Whatever way the soul turns, it is fixed upon sorrows any place except in you, even if fixed upon beautiful things that are outside of you.

The only one who can impart true—that is, eternal—knowledge is Christ.

O that all could live so, but many have not the power!

Must we fear that man despair when his hope is shown to be in God and should not rather despair if in pride he would place it in himself?

Where is the profit in purity of speech that doesn't lead to understanding in a hearer? He who teaches will avoid all words that don't teach.

An unjust law is no law at all.

The Lord of mercy raised me up, that I might not be trodden down to death by passersby, and put me in the nest again.

You have ordered it, and so it is, that every disordered mind should be its own punishment.

*F*or the mysteries which lie hid in Scripture, no one who is content with the simplicity of the faith would curiously sift them.

*T*he world is a great book, of which they that never stir from home read only a page.

*W*ho can map out the various forces at play in one soul? Man is a great depth, O Lord.

*A*nd so it happens that heretics serve usefully for the discovery of the truth.

*L*ove is the beauty of the soul.

Great justice is ascribed to this man, as that he neither wished to keep an adulterous wife, nor could bring himself to punish and expose her.

To give thanks is to acknowledge that all good things come from God, and to thank him for them.

Or must we assume that the bodily senses have their delights, while the mind is not allowed to have any?

Joseph then was not the less His father, because he knew not the mother of our Lord.

Only that really and truly is, which always is in the same way, and not only never changes but is absolutely incapable of changing.

The purpose of all war is peace.

Some men show the effect made on them by the eloquence of a wise man not by applause but by groans and even tears, finally by change of life.

There are wolves within, and there are sheep without.

$\mathcal{J}$ust as within authorities in society the greater is set above the lesser in the order of obedience, so God stands above all others.

$\mathcal{P}$rayer is the greatest stronghold of soul.

$\mathcal{G}$od commands things we cannot do so that we know what to ask of Him. For this is faith itself which obtains by prayer what the law commands.

$\mathcal{A}$nd behold you were within me, and out of myself, and there I searched for you.

Do you wish to rise? Begin by descending. You plan a tower that will pierce the clouds? Lay first the foundation of humility.

Human beings must be humbled,
and God must be exalted.

For what is faith unless it is to believe
what you do not see?

In the absence of justice, what is sovereignty
but organized robbery?

Avenge wrong not with cruelty but with justice in moderation, lest forgiveness without satisfaction harm more the sinner than punishment.

Pray as though everything depended on God. Work as though everything depended on you.

Every man is to be considered our neighbor.

Faith is to believe what you do not yet see; the reward for this faith is to see what you believe.

Thus then by the order and succession of fathers and forefathers, Christ is found to be the Son of David, and the Son of Abraham.

The martyrs vanquished the wicked at the very moment when the latter appeared to be victorious.

Lord, whether prosperity smiles or adversity frowns, let your praise be ever in my mouth.

Nor should we be afraid of being taken to task by those quite unable to understand divine truths.

*I*t is love that asks, that seeks, that knocks,
that finds, and that is faithful
to what it finds.

You owe your conscience to God. But to no one else
do you owe anything more except that you
love one another.

Pride is pregnant with all possible sin.

Grant what Thou commandest and then command
what Thou wilt.

Let us then seek as those who are going to find,
and find as those who are going to go on seeking.

I imagine that none have come here, but they
 who desire to hear, and so I am not speaking
 to hearts that are deaf.

*R*esentment is like taking poison and hoping
 the other person dies.

*O*ne who hears (a teacher) likewise sees those things
 with an inner and individual eye.

*G*uard me, O Holy Spirit,
 that I myself may always be holy.
 Amen.